Tafjordfjell

A Solo Female Wanderer Hiking Guide

Tafjordfjell, A Solo Female Wanderer Hiking Guide. ISBN for paperback 978-1-961878-11-2. Copyright 2024 by Sarah Rowe. For more information about this hiking guide and others, email hi@solofemalewanderer.com

A portion of the proceeds from the sale of this guide is donated to DNT to support their work maintaining the trail system and cabins.

Introduction

The SignaTUR Tafjordfjella goes in between two of the biggest tourist attractions in Fjord Norway, Trollstigen and Geiranger. But in between these tourist attractions there's a mountain area that hasn't yet been discovered by tourists - almost everyone I met on the trip was a Norwegian.

It's easy to fit the long hike into a week long vacation, flying in and out of Ålesund or Molde. The days are much easier and shorter than many of the other SignaTUR hikes, but the views are just as good. It's a fantastic option if you're curious about cabin to cabin tours, ready for something long, but not looking for technically challenging terrain.

Table of Contents

Routes

	Route	Length (km)	
SignaTUR	Grotli to Danskehytta	13.3	
Bonus	Danskehytta to Kaldhusseter	11.2	
Bonus	Kaldhusseter to Reindalseter	13.1	
SignaTUR	Danskehytta to Reindalseter	12.1	
SignaTUR	Reindalseter to Veltdalshytta	11.6	
SignaTUR	Veltdalshytta to Pyttbua	10.2	
Bonus	Veltdalshytta to Torsbu	11.3	
Bonus	Torsbu to Pyttbua	12.2	
SignaTUR	Pyttbua to Vakkerstøylen	7.2	
SignaTUR	Vakkerstøylen to Tjønnebu	13.6	
SignaTUR	Tjønnebu to Grønningsæter	7.3	
Bonus	Billingen to Torsbu and Veltdalshytta	20.4	
Bonus	Reindalseter to Pyttbua	17.6	

The Tafjordfjell SignaTUR is a DNT recommended route that goes from Grotli to Grønningsæter in seven days. If you're looking for a pre-made itinerary, it's a great option - or you can put your own together based on to the point to point hikes

Elevation Gain (m)	Elevation Drop (m)	Time (ut.no)	My rating
634	99	4	Moderate
70	932	4.5	Moderate
702	587	5	Moderate
276	1,025	5.5	Challenging
850	372	5	Challenging
468	494	4	Challenging
324	158	4	Moderate
245	437	4	Moderate
426	725	4.5	Challenging
435	324	5	Challenging
18	597	3	Moderate
683	225	7	Challenging
859	409	6	Challenging

Grotli to Danskehytta

| 13.3 km | 634 meters | 99 meters | 4 hours |
| 8.3 miles | 2,080 feet | 325 feet | Moderate |

The route starts behind Grotli Høyfjellshotell. It took me a few tries to figure out which the correct path was given the number of small paths and roads behind the hotel. Once on the correct trail, the trail climbs gently up for seven kilometers, going mainly over dirt trails with views back towards Breheimen on the left. After seven kilometers, the trail flattens out but becomes very rocky. This section can be hard to spot and requires some rock hopping. There can be snowfields here in early summer, and it can be slick if there's rain. The last kilometer up to the cabin is a steep climb over rocky terrain.

My hiking notes

This is a great first day for the SignaTUR - you can either do it in the early evening after the late bus to Grotli or leave early and have a relaxed day at Danskehytta. Danskehytta is a spacious and comfortable cabin with great views out onto the surrounding mountains and a well stocked provision room.

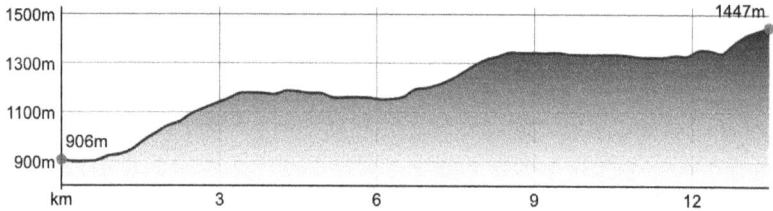

The Tafjordfjell SignaTUR is mostly self-service cabins, but they're much larger than the typical self-service cabin. Most of them have running water during the summers.

Danskehytta to Reindalseter

| 12.1 km | 276 meters | 1,025 meters | 5.5 hours |
| 7.5 miles | 906 feet | 3,363 feet | Challenging |

Start by going north from Danskehytta, following the trail towards Rødalen and then over the dam Heimeste Viksvatnet. The trail continues towards the north, gaining elevation. From here, the trail turns towards the east and crosses an area where there used to be a glacier, Landversbreen. The glacier has sadly melted completely away and is no longer marked on the map. This section is very rocky if the snowfields have melted away, and there are a few sections with chains in the rock to help balance. From here, the trail turns towards the west and goes towards Daurmålsvatnet (Daurmål Lake) and continues over a bridge over the river from the lake to Reindalseter.

Hiking notes

This trail has a few difficult sections with rock hopping, but is doable even by families with kids. I met a family with a five year old who had done this trail in just over six hours. In the case of rain, the trail is slick in the rocky sections, but there's nothing overly technically challenging.

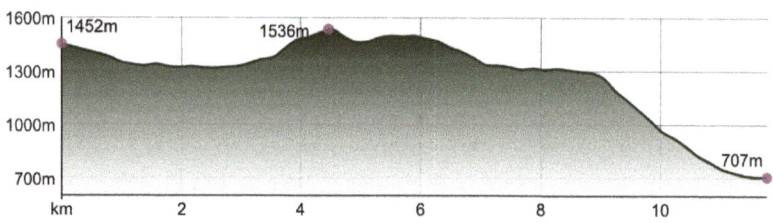

Reindalseter is very popular with families - it's easy to get to from the road, and it has tons of sports equipment (fishing rods, volleyball, etc) on offer

Danskehytta to Kaldhusseter

| 11.2 km | 70 meters | 932 meters | 4.5 hours |
| 6.9 miles | 230 feet | 3,058 feet | Moderate |

This hike is quite a bit of elevation drop over a fairly short distance. The trail starts going towards the northwest and in between two peaks, Fetegga and Helleggi. After that, the trail continues to drop elevation as it goes down through the Kaldhusseterreindalen valley. This section is a very steep drop, and the trail can be rocky in parts. The trail continues towards the east, going alongside a river. There is one section that requires using a chain to help get down a rock face. After eight to nine kilometers of hiking, the trail meets a dirt road that drops very steeply down, then flattens out and goes to the cabin.

<u>Hiking notes</u>

The first section of this hike is relatively easy. I thought it was a straightforward hike without too many technically challenging sections (other than one slightly sketchy section where a slow-melting snowfield had hidden the chain to help get down a rock face).

The drop down to Kaldhusseter on the road was much steeper than I expected. My poles were very handy.

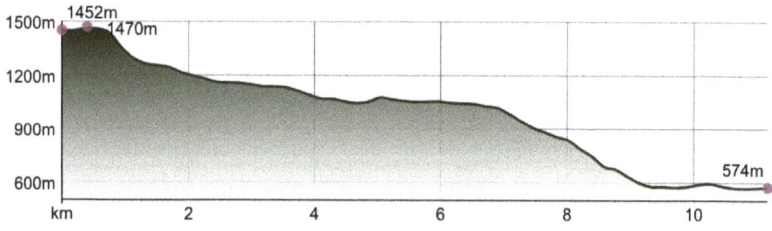

Kaldhusseter is a modern cabin with things like wifi and showers. It's a popular spot for group and school trips.

13

Kaldhusseter to Reindalseter over Zakariasvatnet

| 13.1 km | 702 meters | 587 meters | 5 hours |
| 8.1 miles | 2,303 feet | 1,926 feet | Challenging |

This hike combines two separate hikes, one going from Kaldhusseter to Zakariasvatnet and the other from Zakariasvatnet to Reindalseter. Those sections can also be done individually if you park at Zakariasvatnet. There is no public transportation to Zakariasvatnet, so I've written the description as a cabin to cabin hike rather than as a way to get into the park.

For the first section, from Kaldhusseter to Zakariasvatnet, start by climbing up through a wild birch forest behind the cabin. The initial climb is on dirt trails and easy to follow. After that, the path flattens out slightly and goes under power lines before entering the forest again and continuing the climb. The trail reaches a high point of about 750 meters above sea level here at Flyene. It's worth stopping here and checking out the view point back towards the Tafjord. It was one of the most spectacular views I had on my entire hike.

From here, the trail re-enters the forest and begins to go along the side of the mountain towards Zakariasvatnet. The drop off on the side of the trail is extremely steep, and the trail can be overgrown in parts. It's a difficult trail to maintain, and there are several sections where you will need to use a rope or chain for help crossing the trail.

The trail drops steeply down to a road. Turn right and begin the walk up the road towards the parking lot for Zakariasvatnet. The trail passes by a parking lot and a small cabin that sometimes has waffles for sale, then goes along the lake. The section along the lake is flat, but after the lake, about two kilometers into the hike, there are a few steep but short climbs. The trail continues over a bridge just over the Reindalsfossen waterfall, then has another flat section before a last climb. The last kilometer to Reindalseter is flat, and there are planks down over swampy or wet portions.

Note that Reindalseter often serves dinner at 6pm, an hour earlier than most cabins.

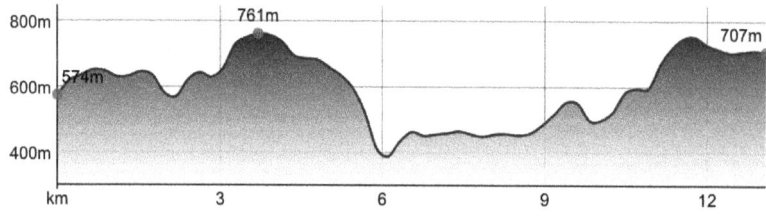

My notes

This section was more tricky than I expected. t I wasn't expecting was how overgrown and steep the section from Kaldhusseter to Zakariasvatnet would be. Because it had rained earlier that day, the path was especially wet and swampy, and that combined with the overgrowth was no fun. I also managed to get caught in a downpour on the road to Zakariasvatnet, so overall, I didn't quite enjoy this as much as I expected. I wouldn't recommend it as an easier or shorter alternative to the route directly from Danskehytta to Reindalseter - I thought it would be easier but longer, but it definitely wasn't.

Reindalseter to Veltdalshytta

| 11.6 km | 850 meters | 372 meters | 5 hours |
| 7.2 miles | 2,789 feet | 1,220 feet | Challenging |

There are two ways that you can get to Veltdalshytta from Reindalseter, either via Rønnebergråsa or via Nedre Veltdalen. I chose to go via Rønnebergråsa, which is part of the historic Fieldfare Route and a more varied hike than Nedre Veltdalen.

The trail starts by climbing up to Hulderkoppen, a bowl with a number of small lakes in it. The trail then goes towards the northeast - be sure not to follow the trial into the Hulderkoppen, which is no longer marked but was still visible when I went. The trail goes over a bridge and then starts to follow the side of the Naushornet mountain until it reaches about 1,300 meters over sea level, about four kilometers into the hike. This section can have snowfields until late in the summer.

The trail continues to climb up to 1,510 meters above sea level, its highest point, and then drops elevation while following the edge of the Langfonna glacier. (Note that the glacier is marked on most maps, but it has almost melted away. I didn't see it coming close to the trail when I hiked.)

The trail drops down from here along a river and then to the side of the Heimste Veltdalsvatnet, a lake. Once I reached the lake, I found it difficult to follow the correct trail, since there are a number of small trails in the area. It took me a couple tries to stay on the correct trail to get the last few hundred meters to Veltdalshytta.

The trail passes by a spur to see Fieldfarehytta, which I strongly recommend.

The trail via Nedre Veltdalen is much flatter with lower elevation gain and loss. It goes past a number of small waterfalls, and there are some sections that can be slippery if there's been rain. Generally, families opt for this one rather than the trail over Rønnebergråsa.

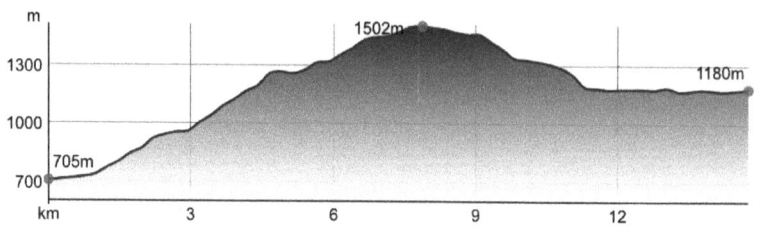

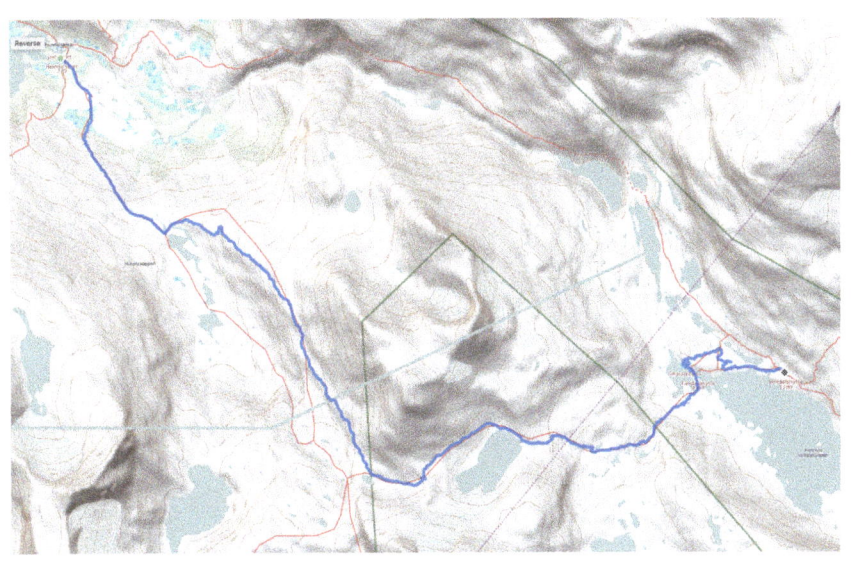

Fieldfarehytta is about a kilometer from Veltdalshytta. It was a hiding spot used by Norwegian resistance fighters working with British secret agents during World War Two, and it's extremely well hidden on the side of the lake. The cabin has been restored to what it looked like during World War Two and is both a museum and a DNT emergency shelter today.

This is a great hike. I had a fantastic time - the trail wasn't wet except for some small parts at the beginning, and the rocky sections weren't overly difficult to hop across. And the views!

I also can't recommend Fieldfarehytta strongly enough. It's incredible to have such a piece of living history, and it's amazing to think about people actually living in the cabin that was there. I can't imagine how they managed an entire winter in such a tiny cabin under such tough conditions. If you're interested in history, definitely consider booking one of the beds and spending the night (although it's much, much less comfortable than Veltdalshytta). You can borrow sleeping bags from Veltdalshytta.

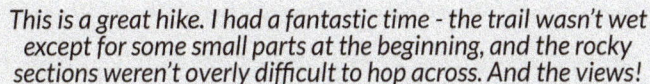

Veltdalshytta to Pyttbua

| 10.2 km | 468 meters | 494 meters | 4 hours |
| 6.4 miles | 1,535 feet | 1,621 feet | Challenging |

The direct route from Veltdalshytta to Pyttbua is relatively flat, and the terrain isn't overly difficult. The trail starts with a short flat section, then turns north and gently climbs up. The trail is mostly dirt and easy to walk along. The trail goes through a high mountain landscape with many small lakes and rivers nearby. After about six kilometers of hiking, the trail meets up with the trail coming from Torsbu. From here, the trail passes Radiovatnet - so named because in 1944, one of the Norwegian resistance members received a radio message from this lake. From here, the trail drops down in sometimes rocky terrain until it crosses over a bridge to Pyttbua.

My notes

This is a short and relatively easy hike - not too rocky, and great views over the nearby mountains and lakes. While there's some elevation gain, it's never steep. It's great if you want to have a slow morning at Veltdalshytta or an early afternoon at Pyttbua.

If you're looking for a longer hike, you can do this route by going over Torsbu. It's longer but not more challenging - the terrain is flat and not too rocky.

m
1500
1300
1100
km
2
4
6
8
10
1515m
1181m
1145m

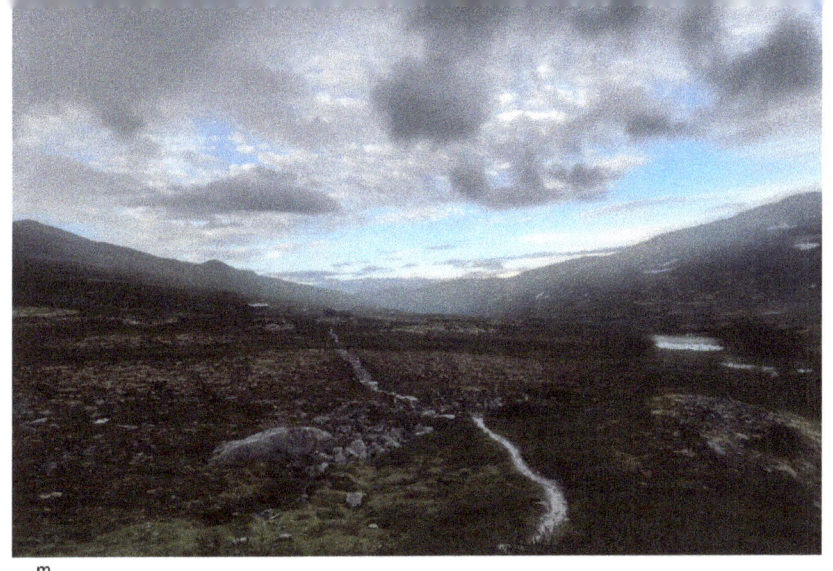

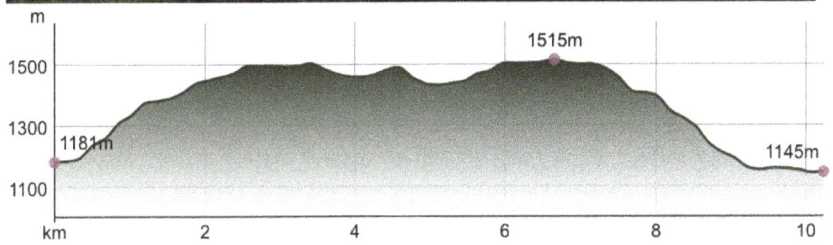

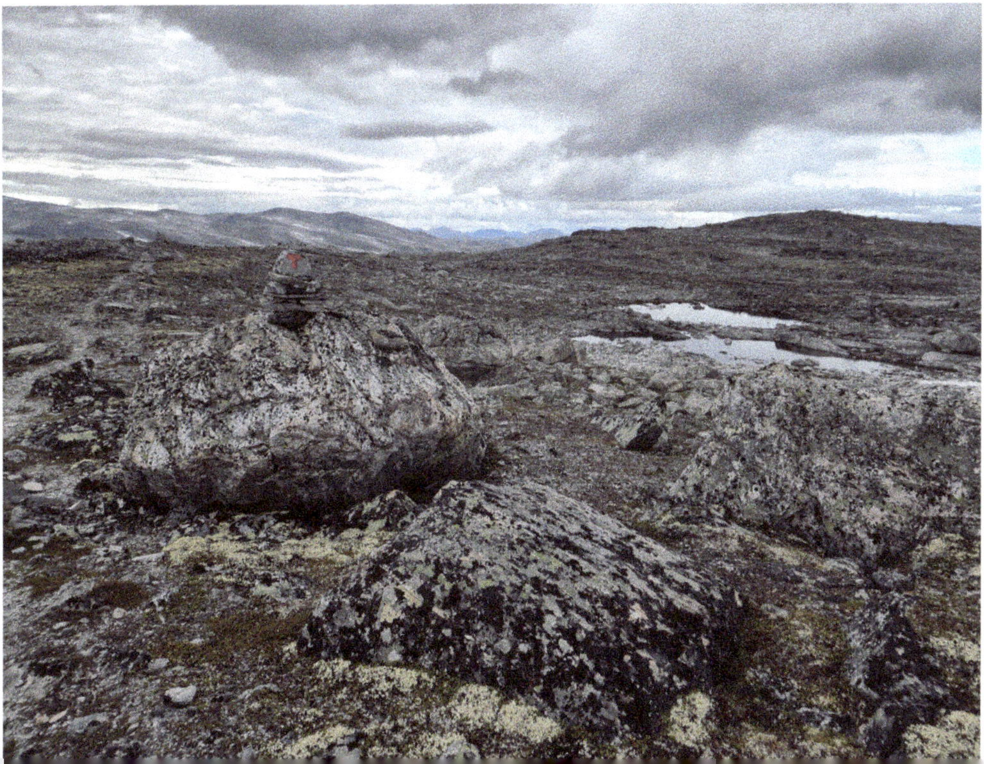

Veltdalshytta to Torsbu

| 11.3 km | 324 meters | 158 meters | 4 hours |
| 7.0 miles | 1,063 feet | 518 feet | Moderate |

This hike starts by going along the Heimste Veitdalsvatnet in front of Veltdalshytta, then continues along the side of Fremste Veltdalsvatnet. There's a small climb here to catch the trail above the lake, then a small drop. After about seven kilometers of hiking, the trail meets up with the trail coming from Billingen and then turns towards the east. It goes through a bowl here with some rocks on the trail, then turns towards the north and reaches Torsbu along the side of the Tordsvatnet.

My hiking notes

This is easy terrain and really flat compared to the days before it. I made great time on this section, but it was also a little less exciting than the prior days. If you like fishing, this can be a great combination day - hike slowly and enjoy the fishing.

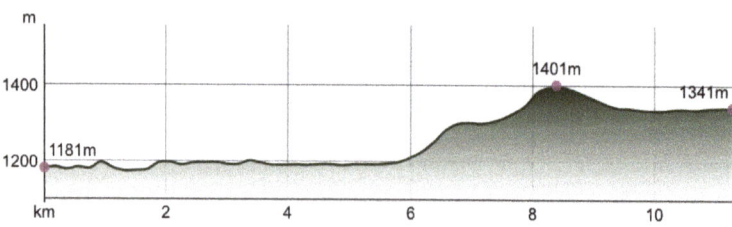

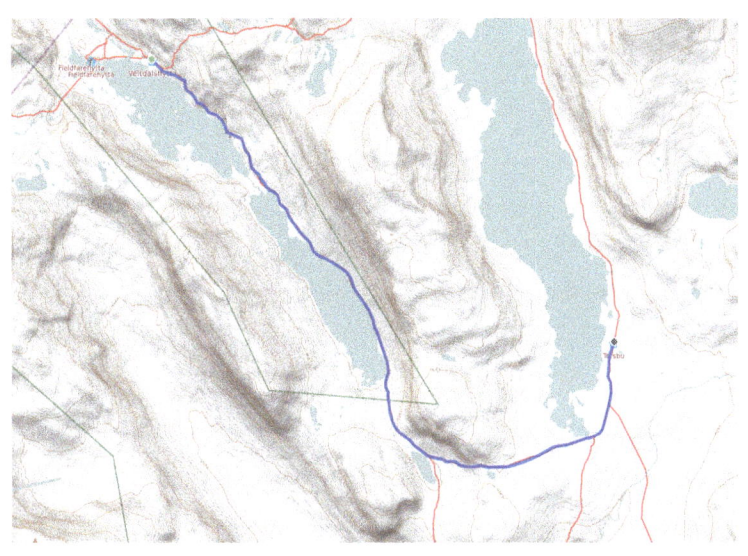

You can fish in the lakes in the park - in fact, fisherpeople often spice up their cabin dinners by catching their own fish to eat

Torsbu to Pyttbua

| 12.2 km | 245 meters | 437 meters | 4 hours |
| 7.6 miles | 804 feet | 1,434 feet | Moderate |

Start by hiking alongside the eastern side of the Tordsvatnet until you reach the end of the lake. From here, the path turns towards the west and climbs slightly until it meets up with the trail from Veltdalshytta to Pyttbua. This section has a little bit of a climb before you go up and over and start the drop down to Pyttbua. There are a few rocks in the trail in this section, but it's generally easy to hike. Make sure to look out for the markings pointing towards the bridge - there was a new bridge put up when I hiked it that did not match the bridge location on my map.

My hiking notes

This was the first time that I had encountered bugs on my hike. Usually it's too cold or windy for them, but the entire way along the Tordsvatnet had a lot of bugs. I made fantastic time mainly because I had to keep moving to keep the bugs from landing on me.

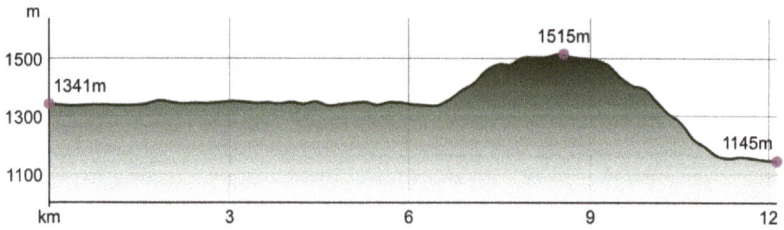

I saw wild reindeer on the this trail! I had never been up close to them before on any of my hikes.

Wild reindeer are highly endangered, and you are legally obligated to give them distance and not disrupt them.

24

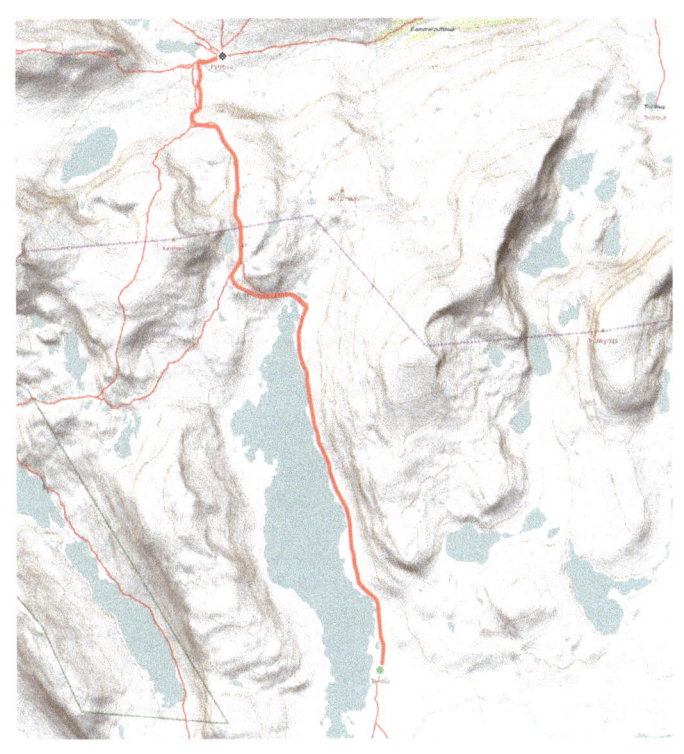

25

Pyttbua to Vakkerstøylen

| 7.2 km | 426 meters | 725 meters | 4.5 hours |
| 4.5 miles | 1,398 feet | 2,379 feet | Challenging |

The trail starts going north behind Pyttbua, climbing up the side of a mountain until it reaches a saddle in between Høgtunga and Lågtunga. This section of the hike has phone service, which neither of the cabins have. It's worth checking the weather and any messages here. From here, the trail starts to drop elevation, first in rocky terrain and then on dirt paths. The trail drops to the side of the lake and then turns north again, going along the lake until it reaches the rowboats.

There are two rowboats, one on each side. You'll have to row across the lake, drop your bags off, tie the second rowboat to the first rowboat, row back with the second boat in tow, tie up the first boat on the southern side of the lake, and then row back in the second boat to Vakkerstøylen. It's three times across the lake, and I found it quite challenging.

The boats are taken in in late September or early October, so if you're planning to hike then, check UT. It's possible to hike around the lake instead of using the rowboats.

My hiking notes

This was much more difficult than I expected. The drop down to the lake is an extremely steep drop - I made much worse time going down than I did going up and frequently had to sit down on the trail. It would be very challenging in wet weather. I also struggled with getting the rowboats to row across the lake - I'm not good at rowing, and one of the downsides of being a solo traveler was that I had to do all of the rowing by myself. I had so much trouble steering the boat that I jumped out of the boat and walked it back to the dock at one point. Fortunately for my shoes, Vakkerstøylen has a very effective drying room with a wood stove.

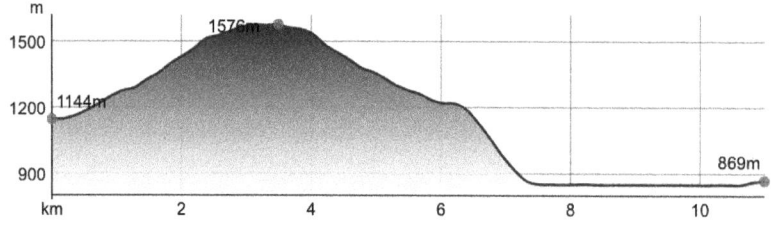

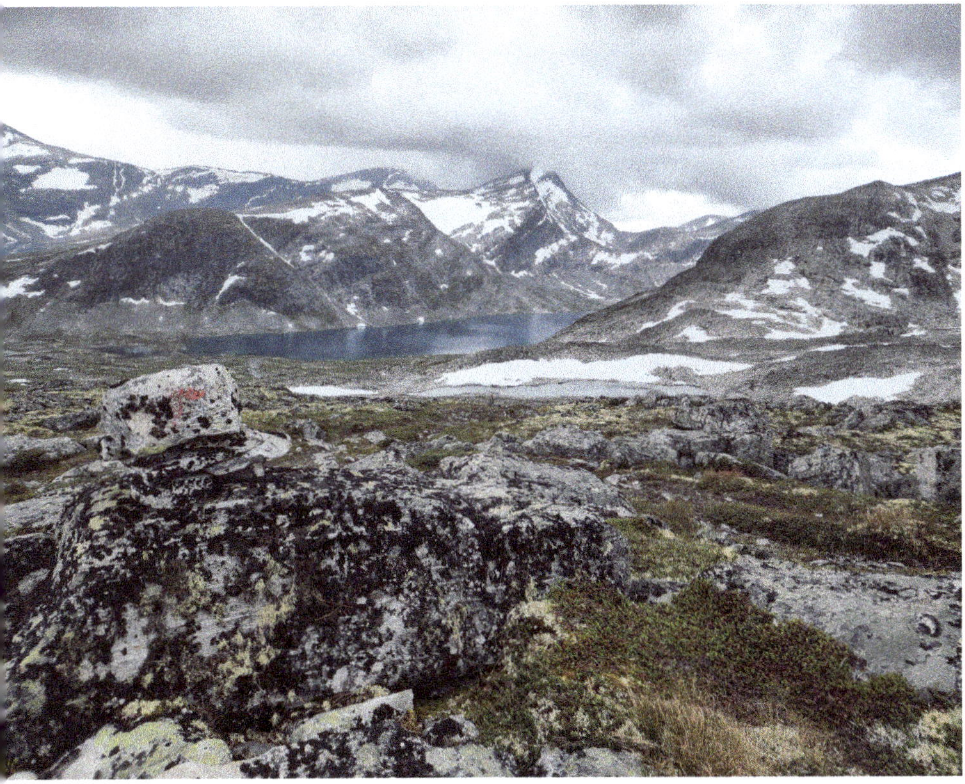

Vakkerstøylen to Tjønnebu

| 13.6 km | 435 meters | 324 meters | 5 hours |
| 8.5 miles | 1,427 feet | 1,063 feet | Challenging |

Start by crossing over the Hånådals River on a bridge right near the cabin. From here, follow the lake and then the river coming from the lake until the trail meets up with the trail coming from Reindalseter. At the junction, take the trial towards the north and follow a new river, the Børrebottelva, up to the Børrebott lake. From here, there's a small climb and then a small drop until before the trail reaches the side of the Illstigvatnet, a lake. Go along the side of the Illstigvatnet, then the trail turns northwest and reaches Tjønnebu on the side of another lake.

My hiking notes

Illstig comes from an old Norwegian word meaning really hard to cross, and that is true. The route along the side of the Illstigvatnet was technically challenging because the terrain drops straight down into the lake, and there were still some patches of snow. I was rock hopping for most of it. There were notes in the guestbook at Tjønnebu from people who had attempted to hike it earlier in the season and had turned back because it was too dangerous.

Tjønnebu is a tiny cabin but very cozy. It has the distinction of being visited by the Norwegian queen, who true to form, signed in in the protocol book – the page is now framed on the wall. It also has the coziest toilet of any cabin I have been to, including a lovely rug and plenty of artwork on the walls. It's unserviced, so you'll need to bring all your own food and carry out all trash.

m
1179m
1100
987m
900
870m
km
3
6
9
12

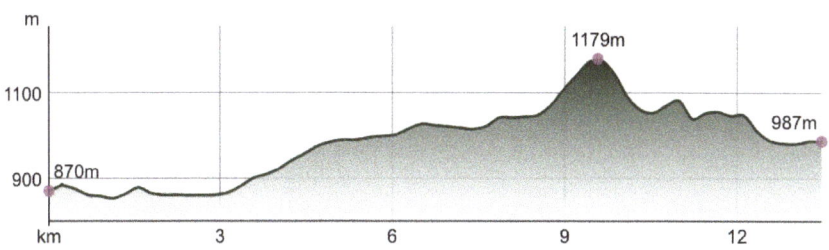

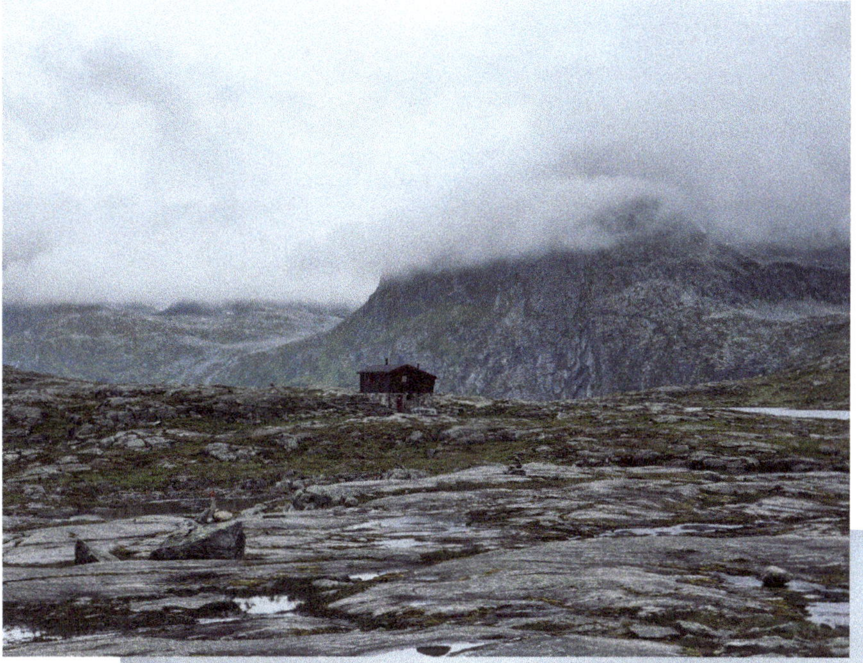

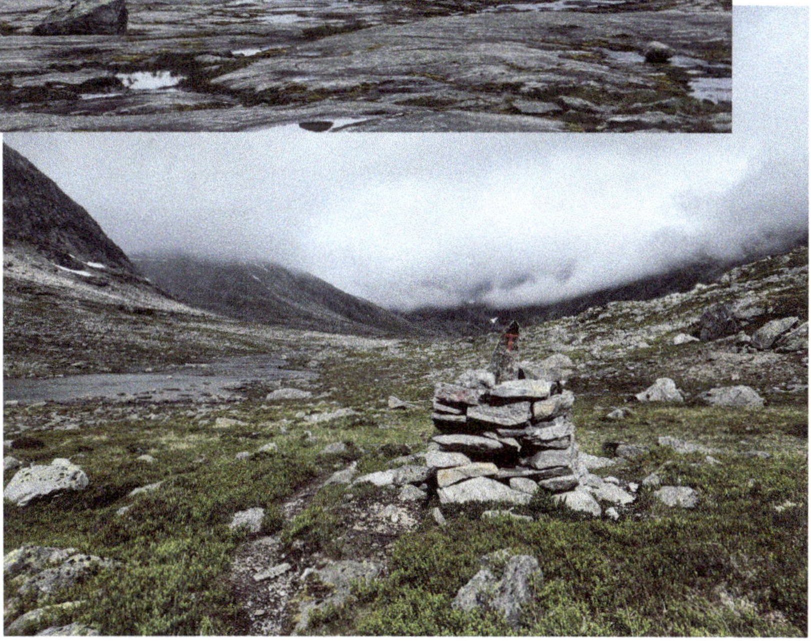

Tjønnebu to Grønningsæter

7.3 km
4.5 miles

18 meters
59 feet

597 meters
1,959 feet

3 hours
Moderate

This is an easy drop out of the national park and can be combined with the hike from Vakkerstøylen to Tjønnebu. Follow the trail as it starts going north, then curves northwest, going through the valley and dropping elevation. Eventually, the trail starts to go alongside the Steindalselva on the south side, turning slightly south before sharply dropping elevation and ending at the Grønningsæter parking lot.

There is usually a bus between Valldal and Åndalsnes that stops at Grønningsæter. I did the route in 2024, when the Trollstigen road was closed, so I had to call a taxi to Grønningsæter. It is possible to hike to Valldal from Grønningsæter, but it's 21 kilometers along the road.

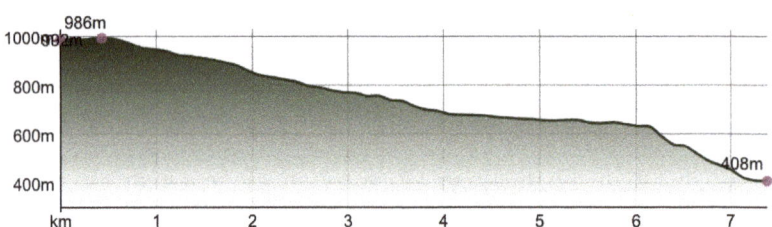

This route was as easy as it looked on the map. It's a straightforward trail. The only downside for me was that the bus wasn't running, so I had to overcome my stubbornness and break down and get a taxi back to Valldal. There are plenty of spectacular waterfalls on the way.

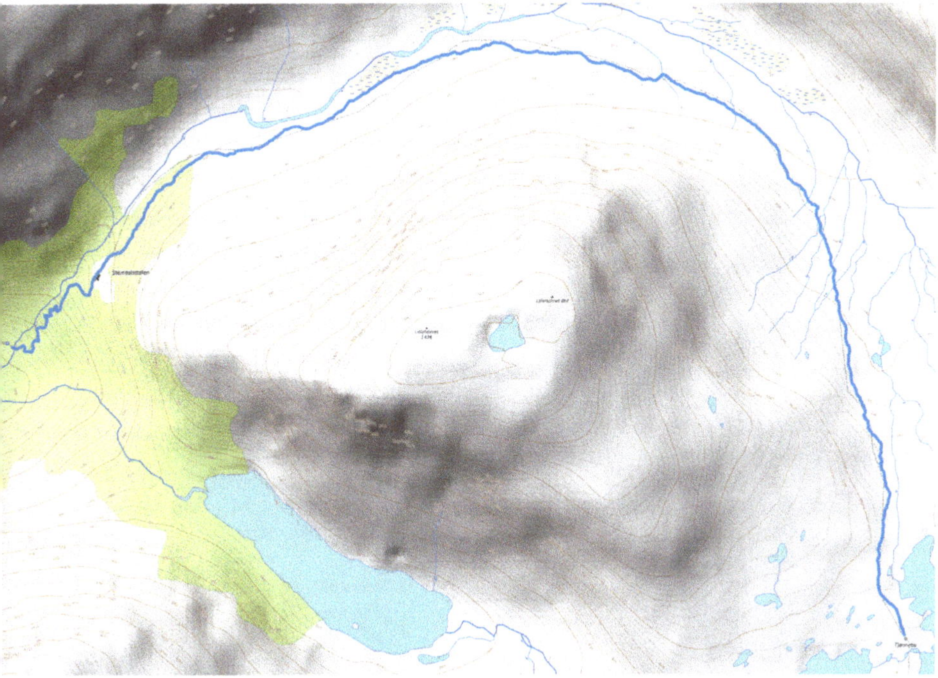

31

Billingen to Veltdalshytta

20.4 km
12.7 miles

683 meters
2,241 feet

225 meters
738 feet

7 hours
Challenging

This trail is another option if you want to enter into the Tafjordfjell from Billingen rather than from Grotli. They are on the same highway and have similar public transit options, but if you are driving your own car, it is likely easier to park at Billingen. From the highway, RV 15, follow the local road up through a series of farms before catching the trail at the top eastern switchback of the local road. From here, follow the Torda river on the west side up until you reach a private cabin, Tverrådalshytta. From here, keep going north towards Kupevatnet. From here, the trail continues to the north, then goes along the Veltdalsvatnet to Veltdalshytta.

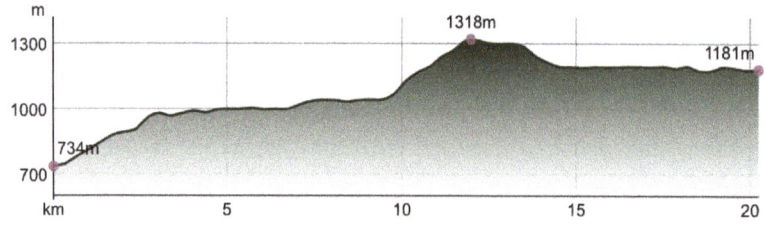

33

Reindalseter to Pyttbua

| 17.6 km | 859 meters | 409 meters | 6 hours |
| 10.9 miles | 2,818 feet | 1,342 feet | Challenging |

Start by going north from Reindalseter. The trail runs along the north side of the Tverrelva, a river. There are several side rivers that have year-round bridges over them in this section. Keep going as the trail gradually turns towards the east, then passes the trail to Vakkerstøylen.

The trail crosses over its high point here, between Isholfjellet (mountain) and Puttegga (mountain). There are snowfields here until late in the summer, so I recommend poles. The snow may be icy from melt and refreezing, especially early in the season.

The trail turns towards the east and then more south, going along the north side of Botnvatnet ("the Botn lake"). From here, the trail gradually flattens out and arrives at Pyttbua.

My notes

This hike is one of the legs of the Reindalseter to Veltdalshytta to Pyttbua to Reindalsheter hike. That route has classic high mountain terrain and can be spectacular, but it's more difficult than some of the other hikes in the Tafjordfjell.

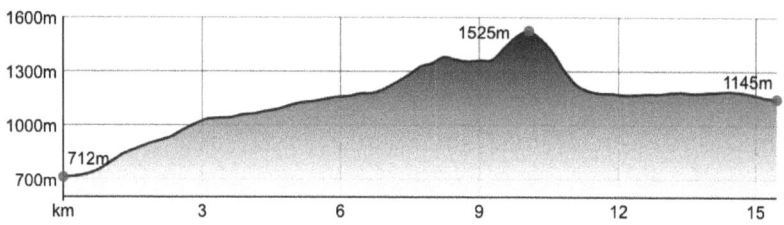

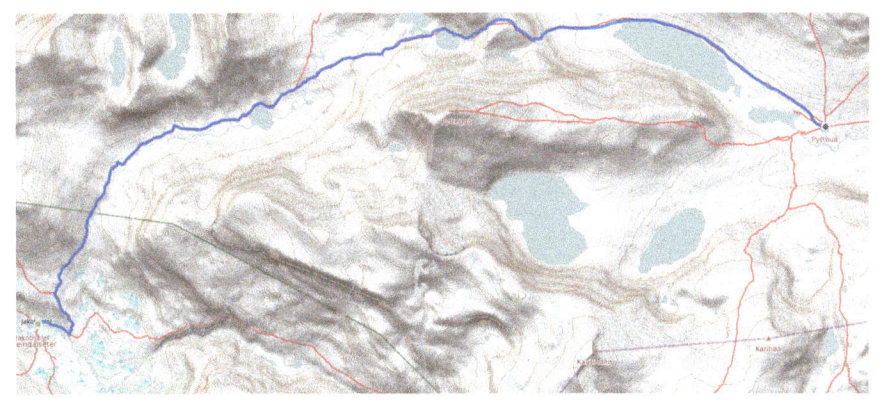

35

Logistics

Getting There and Back

There are a few different ways to get to the Tafjordfjell. From various nearby cities:

- From Valldal: take a taxi, bus, or walk to Grønningsæter, then hike in to Tjønnebu. Note that this bus didn't run in summer 2024 because Trollstigen was closed for potential rockslides - check entur.no before you use this route.

- From Ålesund: take the bus to either Valldal or Åndalsnes and go from there, depending on what portion of the hike you'd like to start. I recommend the bus to Valldal - it runs every couple of hours and has a very scenic route.

- From Åndalsnes: take the bus to Grønningsæter, then hike in to Tjønnebu.

- From Dombås: take the train to Lesjaskog, then take a taxi or hike in to Kabben, where you can start a short hike to Vakkerstøylen (6km along the lake).

- From Lom: take the bus to either Billingen or Grotli. The bus runs twice a day and must be booked at least fifteen minutes in advance.

- From Stryn: take the bus to either Billingen or Grotli. The bus runs twice a day and must be booked at least fifteen minutes in advance.

Supplies

Almost all of the cabins on the Tafjordfjell are self-service cabins. DNT Sunnmøre maintains these cabins, and I found that all of them had well-stocked provision rooms and plenty of supplies.

There are no good drop points or stores easily accessible from the Tafjordfjell, so I recommend bringing everything you need. It's easiest to get things from one of the towns or cities before you start the Tafjordfjell. My recommendation would be to pick up a few things to spice up the meals in the cabins - cheese for putting on top of sandwiches, spreads for pancakes, or fresh fruit, for example. Self-service cabin food gets the job done, but it can get a little boring.

Camping

Norway has some of the most permissive laws in the world around camping. Norway has a law called the Allemannsretten that guarantees the ability of people to explore and experience nature, even in privately owned areas, as long as you're in uncultivated land. Once you're in the wilderness, you may camp in any area, as long as you're at least 150 meters away from the nearest inhabited house or cabin. Note that the 150 meters applies to DNT cabins as well.

Campfires are prohibited everywhere in Norway from April 15 to September 15, except in specifically marked areas in camping sites and by the coast. You will need to bring a gas stove to cook, and in the case of intense drought, even gas stoves may be banned.

The Tafjordfjell is not overly rocky, so there are many good spots for camping. Most of the people I met on the trip stayed in the cabins rather than camped since it was mostly self-service cabins, but I did meet some people camping.

Planning Resources

yr.no is the best resource for weather in Norway. It allows you to hike by specific cabin or mountaintop, with the weather for that particular point rather than the overall area. It's available in English.

Senorge.no shows the current and historic weather conditions for any point in Norway. It's very useful for checking the amount of snow remaining for summer hikes, as well as seeing if it's rained recently.

enTUR is the best source for information on public transit. Google Maps does not show complete, accurate information for Norway.

Ut.no, both the app and the website, shows all of the cabins and trails in Norway. It's unfortunately only in Norwegian, but is the best source of information on cabins and trails. You can download offline maps by going to "Profil" and then "Mine offline-kart" on the app.

Varsom.no shows storm and avalanche warnings. It's available in English.

If you're stopping by a DNT office before going hiking, you can pick up a planleggingskart, or planning map. These aren't usable for hiking but are great for planning.

Packing List

In total, the gear below should weigh 7 to 12 kilograms (15 to 25 pounds).

Gear

- ☐ 46-55 liter hiking backpack with a rain shield
- ☐ Maps and compass:
- ☐ Hiking poles: *optional for the Tafjordfjell, but helpful for some of the steeper descents*
- ☐ Duct tape
- ☐ Dry bags for packing
- ☐ First aid kit

Clothing

- ☐ Hiking boots
- ☐ Trail runners: *these are optional, but I use mine to give my feet a break from heavy hiking boots. They worked well on the easier days (Tjønnebu to Grønningsæter, Danskehytta to Kaldhusseter)*
- ☐ Rain pants and optional gaiters: *in myr or grasses, the water from plants nearby will soak into your pants if you don't have rain pants or gaiters.*
- ☐ Rain jacket
- ☐ Windbreaker: *it's frequently misting in the mornings, so if you don't like hiking in your rain jacket, bring a lighter weight jacket to hike in*
- ☐ Wool socks, two pairs: *I use one pair of socks for hiking and one pair for the cabin.*
- ☐ Hiking shorts (optional): *it may be warm enough to hike in shorts , but it's very year dependent.*
- ☐ Hiking pants or long underwear to layer under rain pants
- ☐ Wool sweater
- ☐ Extra warm jacket
- ☐ Two sports bras and two pairs of underwear
- ☐ Hat and gloves
- ☐ Two hiking shirts

Cabin Supplies

☐ Mini towel

☐ DNT key: *all of the cabins except for Torsbu were unlocked, but I always bring my DNT key just in case*

☐ Sengetøy (sheet set) or sleep liner: *the blankets on the beds are not washed in between guests. You need to bring your own sheets to keep things clean*

☐ Toilet shoes: *about half of the cabins have outdoor toilets, and this keeps you from having to put potentially wet hiking boots back on*

☐ Sleep mask: *there are good curtains in the cabins, but it never gets dark*

Food and Drink

☐ Thermos for hot drinks

☐ Small water bottle or cup: *there are plenty of rivers and streams to fill up in on the way; you can drink the water as long as there's not active sheep grazing. (Don't drink straight from the stream near Vakkerstøylen.)*

☐ Candy and snacks

☐ Plastic bag for sandwiches

Tech

☐ Phone: *I recommend downloading UT, YR, and Hyttebetaling before your hike. You may also want to screenshot bed reservations and info for the cabins, since there's limited phone service*

☐ Battery pack

☐ Chargers: *many of the cabins only have USB classic charging outlets. If you have a phone with a USB-C charging port, you will want to bring a USB to USB-C charger.*

Other

☐ ID and credit cards: *all of the cabins are payable with the Hyttebetaling app, so there's no need to bring cash*

☐ Sunglasses and sunscreen: *almost the entire hike is unshaded, so if it's sunny, you'll need sunscreen*

☐ Toiletries

☐ Tiny shovel and toilet paper

☐ Extra plastic bags

Some Handy Norwegian Words

Almost all Norwegians speak perfect English. That said, there are times where it's handy to be able to read signs, the weather, or the map.

Hiking and the map

Bratt/meget bratt: steep/very steep

Breen: the glacier

Dalen: the valley

Grusvei: a gravel path

Luftig: steep drop offs on the side of the trail

Kvistet: marked (used for ski trails)

Merket: marked (used for summer trails)

Mobildekning: phone service

Myr: a swampy, wet land covering

Nord, sor, ost, vest: north, south, east, west

Skog: forest

Stein: rocky

Steinur: rocky patches to hike over

Tind/tinden: peak

Vadested: a place that requires wading

Vannet: the water

Varder: cairns

Vatnet: the lake

Vegen/veien: the road

Weather

Bris: breeze

Flom: flood

Lettskyet: barely cloudy

Lyn: lighting

Nedbør: precipitation

Nysnø: new snow (no icy cover yet)

Regn: rain

Weather continued

Skyet: cloudy

Snø: snow

Sol: sun

Soloppgang, solnedgang: sunrise, sunset

Strynregen: very heavy rain

Tåkete: foggy

Torden: thunder

Things in provision rooms

Bønnemix: mixed beans

Erter: peas

Fullkorn: whole grain

Gryte: stew

Hermetikk: shelf-stable boxes

Kaffe: coffee

Kanel: cinnamon

Kokemalt: coffee that needs to be cooked in a kettle

Kjeks: biscuits

Kjøtt: meat

Knekkebrød: crispbread

Kokk uten lokk: cook without a lid

Kylling: chicken

Lapskaus: a Norwegian stew of potatoes and meat

Legg til: add to (e.g. "legg til vann" = "add water")

Linser: lentils

Melkepulver: milk powder (reconstitute with water)

Ost: cheese

Pannekake: pancakes

Food continued

Potetmos: mashed potatoes

Rein: reindeer

Ror godt: stir well

Smør: butter

Sodd: a high calorie stew of pork, potatoes, and some vegetables

Sukker: sugar

Svine: pork

Syltetøy: jam

Turmat: dehydrated hiking food

Vann: water

Cabins

Betjent: serviced (a lodge)

Selvbetjent: self-service (a cabin without staff but with a provision room)

Ubetjent: unserviced (a cabin with beds, propane, and wood, but no food)

Drikkevann: drinking water

Forhåndsbestilt: booked in advance

Hyttefelt: a collection of cabins

Protokoll: the book you have to sign when you arrive at a cabin

Sikringshytta: the smaller, secondary cabin

Using the Cabins

One of the most amazing things about hiking in Norway is the national cabin network. The Norwegian Trekking Association (DNT) maintains a network of more than 600 cabins spread across the country. Cabins come in three grades:

Betjent (serviced):

These aren't cabins but full lodges. You'll have a three course meal for dinner, a buffet breakfast with a place to fill your thermos, showers and drying rooms for clothes, and often indoor toilets.

Dinners are served family style, where the staff will bring out giant tureens of soup for a first course, then usually some kind of meat and potatoes, then individual desserts. There's more than enough food for everyone - but make sure to book ahead and alert the cabin if you're vegetarian or have dietary restrictions.

The family style dinners mean that you have to go to an assigned dinner time. There's usually assigned seating as well, which means that you'll be put with other travelers. People strike up conversations and ask where you've hiked from and are happy to speak English.

Serviced cabins have electricity but a limited number of outlets, often only in the common areas.

Reindalseter is the only serviced cabin in the Tafjordfjell.

Selvbetjent (self-service)

Self-service cabins are unique to Norway. They're generally smaller than staffed cabins, but come fully stocked with a provision room, wood for the fireplace, gas for cooking, and cooking supplies. Some have electricity, but it's usually from a solar panel. You usually have to fetch and boil water from a nearby water source, although the larger cabins in the Tafjordfjell have running water during the summer season.

The self-service cabins operate on the honor system. To pay for your stay, use the Hyttebetaling app. The app allows you to keep a list of all the supplies you've used and then pay with credit card when you get back into phone service.

Self-service cabins usually need to be unlocked with the DNT key, but most of the cabins in the Tafjordfjell are left unlocked during the summer season.

Ubetjent (unserviced)

These are just like self-service cabins, except that there is no provision room with food. Tjønnebu is the only unserviced cabin in the Tafjordfjell.

Cabin Etiquette:

When you arrive at an unserviced or self-service cabin, the first thing to do is to unlock the cabin and then take off your shoes. No outdoor shoes are allowed in the cabin to help keep it clean. After that, fill in your information in the besøksprotokoll, a horizontal blue book that asks where you came from, where you're going, and your membership information. After that, you have the right to use the cabin. I generally first start a fire if the cabin is cold, then fetch water to heat up for dinner.

When you leave the cabin in the morning, you'll need to clean up. That means washing all of the dishes, cleaning out the ashes in the fireplace, bringing in fresh wood for the fire, washing (not just sweeping) the floors in the bedroom and common areas, and any other tidying.

If you're camping , you can still use the cabin during the day if you pay for a day visit ("dagsbesøk"). Make sure to sweep up and wash the floors after yourself.

It's not necessary to book in advance for any of the cabins - if you arrive at the cabin, you'll have a place to sleep, though it might be on a mattress on the floor if it's really busy. I generally don't book cabins in advance so that I have the most flexibility possible to change hiking plans based on the weather.

Joining DNT:

Joining DNT gives you a discount on staying the night at the cabin. It pays for itself with a couple of nights, especially if you qualify for a youth or senior membership. The blog has instructions on how to join and get your membership number online, or you can stop by any DNT office in Norway.

While the DNT key isn't strictly necessary on this hike, since the cabins other than Torsbu are unlocked, I recommend picking one up anyway.

Cooking at the cabin:

There are stoves and cooking supplies in the cabins. The food that you'll generally find breaks down into four categories:

Breakfast: knekkebrød, oatmeal, pancake mix, leverposti (liver spread), jam and chocolate spread, mackerel in tomatoes, butter, jam, and honey

Dinner: fish soup, peas and carrots, mashed potato mix, lapskaus, rice, bacalo, boxed mixes for Pasta di Parma and Chili Con Carne, pasta, reindeer meatballs, dry red lentils, and crushed tomatoes

Snacks and dessert: chocolate pudding, vanilla sauce , canned fruit in syrup, and biscuits

Misc things: dried hiking food, coffee, tea, hot chocolate, currant drink mix, hiking snacks like knekkebrød sandwiches, sugar, cinnamon

Each cabin has a different selection of food, and if you're late in the season, certain items might be eaten up. If you're vegetarian or gluten-free, make sure to have your own backup food.

My challenge with cooking at self-service cabins is finding something to bring for lunch the next day. I really load up on breakfast, often mixing vanilla sauce or jam into my oatmeal for the extra calories. I take two or three packages of freeze dried food with me to eat on the trail, in case there isn't shelf-stable cheese and knekkebrød for lunch.

Since it's almost all self-service cabins on this route, you may want to bring along some extras to spice up your meals. I sometimes bring cheese or sausage for lunch, or for dinner, pesto and parmesan cheese on top of pasta.

Fjellvettreglene (Norwegian Mountain Code)

The Norwegian Mountain Code contains the guidelines for having a safe trip in the Norwegian mountains. They're considered an important part of Norwegian cultural heritage and were introduced after a spate of fatal accidents in 1950.

1. Plan your trip and inform others about the route you have selected.

2. Adapt the planned routes according to ability and conditions.

3. Pay attention to the weather and the avalanche warnings.

4. Be prepared for bad weather and frost, even on short trips.

5. Bring the necessary equipment so you can help yourself and others.

6. Choose safe routes. Recognize avalanche terrain and unsafe ice.

7. Use a map and a compass. Always know where you are.

8. Don't be ashamed to turn around.

9. Conserve your energy and seek shelter if necessary.

Cabin Overview

Cabin	Cabin Type	Total beds	Number bookable	Power
Grotli	Private hotel	120	120	Yes, 220 volt
Danskehytta	Self-service	26	22	Yes, 12 volt
Kaldhusseter	Self-service	30	26	Yes, 220 volt
Reindalseter	Serviced	76	76	Yes, 220 volt
Veltdalshytta	Self-service	51	24	Yes, 12 volt
Jakobselet	Unserviced	7	7	N
Fieldfarehytta	Emergency shelter	3	3	N
Pyttbua	Self-service	51	31	Yes, 12 volt
Torsbu	Self-service	14	6	Yes, 12 volt
Vakkerstøylen	Self-service	24	16	Yes, 12 volt
Tjønnebu	Unserviced	8	5	N

	Phone Service	Drying Room	Shower	Other Notes
	Y	N	Y	Book in advance; can sell out
	Minimal	N	N	In winter, the secondary cabin (sikringshytta) is used
	Y	N	Y	Modern cabin with wifi
	N	Y	Y	
	N	Y	N	
	N	N	N	Unserviced alternative to Reindalseter; must book whole cabin
	N	N	N	Also a museum. To stay here, you have to pick up sleeping bags from Veltdalshytta. No facilities
	N	Y	N	
	N	N	N	Smallest of the self-serviced cabins in the Tafjordfjell. Run by DNT Oslo, not DNT Sunnmøre like the others
	N	Y	N	
	N	N	N	Has DNT's coziest toilet

Sarah Rowe has solo hiked more than 3,500 kilometers across 21 countries, with a focus on Norway and Austria. She's completed six of DNT's SignaTUR long hikes, including the Massiv route.

When she's not out in the mountains, she's drinking coffee, writing about hiking on her blog, Solo Female Wanderer, or planning the next adventure.

She lives in the northeastern United States, two kilometers from the Appalachian Trail.

Questions or comments? You can reach her at
sarah@solofemalewanderer.com.